SPORTS GREAT
BO JACKSON

Ron Knapp

— Sports Great Books —

Enslow Publishers, Inc.

44 Fadem Road	PO Box 38
Box 699	Aldershot
Springfield, NJ 07081	Hants GU12 6BP
USA	UK

Library of Congress Cataloging-in-Publication Data:

Knapp, Ron.
    Sports Great Bo Jackson / Ron Knapp.
        p. cm. — (Sports great books)
    Includes index.
    Summary: Traces the life story of the star athlete Bo Jackson
and discusses his double career in professional baseball and
football.
    ISBN 0-89490-281-4
    1. Jackson, Bo. 1962- —Juvenile literature. 2.
Athletes—United States—Biography—Juvenile literature. 3.
Football players—United States—Biography—Juvenile literature.
4. Baseball players—United States—Biography—Juvenile literature.
5. Los Angeles Raiders (Football team)—Juvenile literature.
6. Kansas City Royals (Baseball team)—Juvenile literature.
[1. Jackson, Bo, 1962- . 2. Football players. 3.
Baseball players. 4. Afro-Americans—Biography.] I. Title.
II. Series.
GV697.J27K58   1990
92—dc20
[796'.092]
[B]   89-29059
                               CIP
                               AC

Printed in the United States of America

10 9 8 7 6

Illustration Credits: Auburn Athletic Department: pp. 6, 10, 21, 22, 26, 29, 33;
Auburn University Child Study Center: p. 32; Rob Brown: pp. 49, 54, 57;
Courtesy of Detroit Tigers: p. 43; Courtesy Kansas City Royals: pp. 12, 19, 34, 38,
40, 42, 45, 59; Joe McNally/*Sports Illustrated*: p. 16; Copyright The Topps
Company, Inc.: pp. 47, 51; University of Iowa Athletic Department: p. 8.

Cover Photo: Rob Brown

Contents

— Sports Great Books —

Chapter 1

No one at Auburn University had ever seen anyone like Bo Jackson. He was big. He was fast. He was strong. He could play baseball and football like nobody else. By 1985, Bo already had three fine years at Auburn. He wanted his last year to be his best.

The Auburn Tigers started off the football season with a bang by stomping Southwest Louisiana 49–7. Jackson gained 290 yards and scored four touchdowns. He had two more touchdowns and 205 yards the next week when Auburn beat Southern Mississippi. In just the first two games of the 1985 season, Bo Jackson had almost 500 yards. After six games, he had eleven touchdowns and 1,233 yards. That meant he had an average of more than 200 yards per game.

But some people still were not impressed. Bo had a lot of talent, but did he really have the "guts" to be a truly great player? When Auburn played Tennessee, Jackson left the game early because of a sore knee. "Nothing serious," he said. "It just hurts." Some fans thought he was too easy on himself. They didn't think a sore knee should keep him from playing.

Jackson got a chance to show his talent—and his guts—in the last game of the season. The Auburn Tigers were battling the Crimson Tide of Alabama. Unfortunately, he was in bad shape. A rough tackle had given him a pair of broken ribs, a very painful injury. It hurt him just to breathe. Many fans didn't expect Jackson to play, but he surprised them. It was the last game of the season, and, since he was a senior, the last

Bo Jackson had four exciting seasons as a running back for the Auburn Tigers.

time he would ever play for the Auburn Tigers. Bo wanted to go out with a bang.

It was a very courageous performance. Even with a pair of broken ribs, Bo carried the ball thirty-one times and gained 142 yards. With time running out, Auburn was ahead 23–22. But Alabama's Van Tiffin kicked a 52-yard field goal on the last play of the game. Alabama won 25–23. Bo and the rest of the Auburn Tigers walked sadly off the field, but they knew they had given it everything they had. Finally, everybody knew that Bo Jackson was more than just a talented athlete. He was tough, too.

Once the season was over, it was time for the Heisman Trophy to be awarded. Each year, this trophy is given to the best college football player in the country. Many fans thought the 1985 award should go to Jackson. He had finished the season with 1,786 yards and seventeen touchdowns. But 1985 had been a big year for other players, too. Chuck Long, Iowa's quarterback, had completed 231 passes. Michigan State's Lorenzo White had gained more yards than anybody. Robbie Bosco of Brigham Young had thrown twenty-eight touchdown passes.

But, after Bo's game against Alabama, most of the sportswriters decided that Jackson was the best college football player in the country. He had talent — and he was tough. He beat out Long, White, and Bosco for the 1985 Heisman Trophy.

After four great years at Auburn, Jackson's college football career was over. But that didn't mean he was finished with the sport. He began to think about playing professional football in the National Football League.

The NFL teams have a meeting to divide up the best college players. It is called the college draft. Bo was drafted by the Tampa Bay Buccaneers. They offered him $500,000 a

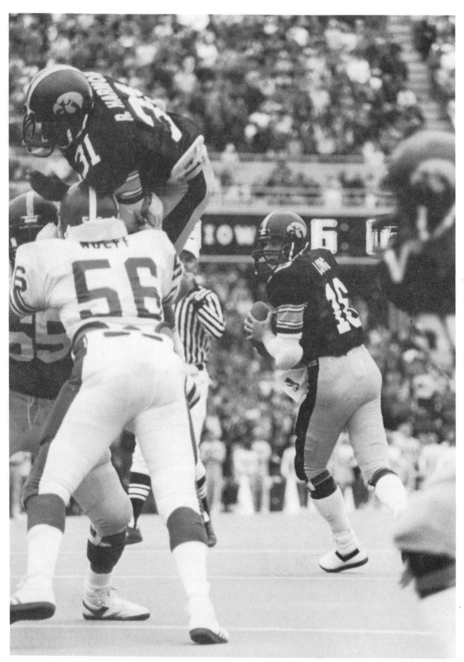

Chuck Long, Iowa's quarterback (#16), also had a great year in 1985. He and Bo Jackson were both contenders for the Heisman Trophy.

year to play for them. Most people expected him to sign right away, but they had forgotten that Bo Jackson could do more than just play football. He was also a great baseball player.

In high school, Bo didn't have time for baseball practice because he was also on the track team. But even without practicing, he hit twenty home runs his senior year to tie a national record. Bo was as fast as he was powerful. At Auburn, he hit a one-hopper to the pitcher, then beat the ball to first base for a single. Nobody had ever seen that kind of speed before.

Even though he was a star baseball player for Auburn, Jackson had devoted most of his time and energy to football. In four years at college, he had only played in eighty-nine baseball games. That didn't bother the Kansas City Royals major league baseball team. They offered him about $200,000 a year to play baseball instead of football.

Bo had to decide whether to play football for the Tampa Bay Buccaneers or baseball for the Kansas City Royals. He knew he was lucky. He could become a rich man by playing either one. Most fans thought he would give up baseball for football. After all, he was the best college football player in the country, and he could make more than twice as much money by playing football for the Buccaneers.

What was it going to be—baseball or football? Bo made a joke about his decision. He said he was going to pick the sport he loved the most. "And what I really love the most," he said, "is hunting and fishing."

While the Buccaneers and Royals awaited his decision, Jackson worked with children at Auburn. That was something he loved to do almost as much as football or baseball or hunting and fishing. In his classes, he studied child development. In his spare time, he volunteered to work with kids at the Auburn Child Study Center. He played with the children and gave them advice. "Don't run life too fast," he said. "You only have one." Obey your parents, he told them. Stay out of trouble. The kids liked Bo. They knew he cared about them.

But, of course, everybody knew Bo Jackson wasn't ready to make a career out of working with kids. He was going to be a professional athlete — possibly a superstar — but would he be

When he wasn't busy with football or track, Bo played on the Auburn baseball team.

a running back or an outfielder? Finally he made his decision—and it was a surprise. "I'm lucky to have played football as long as I did," he said. "Now it's time for what I love to do." He signed with the Kansas City Royals to play baseball. The Tampa Bay Buccaneers couldn't believe it. It looked like Bo Jackson's football days were over.

Jackson didn't go to Kansas City right away. Instead, he was sent to Memphis, Tennessee, to play on a Double-A minor league team. He would get a lot of practice there batting, throwing, and fielding. Bo played all summer for the Memphis Chicks. Then, in September, he got his chance to come to Kansas City and play for the Royals in the major leagues.

On his first day in Kansas City, a coach pitched him balls for batting practice. Bo slammed them up the middle, down the lines, and over the fences. His hits were zinging all over the park. The coach jumped out of the way and said, "This guy is scary." Once again, Bo's speed helped him turn ordinary ground balls into base hits. Before the infielders could get the ball to first base, he was already there. In only his seventh game in the major leagues, he hit a 475-foot home run. It was one of the longest balls ever hit at Royals Stadium.

By the spring of 1987, Jackson was the Royals' regular left fielder. It looked like he was on his way to a great baseball career.

Then he started thinking about doing something hardly anybody had ever done before. Even though he loved baseball, he decided he missed football. But he didn't want to give up baseball. He wanted to play them both. "Hey, maybe this isn't so crazy," he said. "Bo Jackson succeeding in two sports." And so he signed a contract to play football for the Los Angeles Raiders. He would get paid a million and a half dollars each year to play football after the baseball season was over.

Baseball is played in the spring and summer, and most of the football season is played in the fall and winter. Bo figured he'd have plenty of time to be on both teams, the Royals and the Raiders.

When the 1987 baseball season was over, Jackson took off

Bo surprised almost everybody by signing with the Kansas City Royals to play baseball.

his Royals baseball uniform and put on his Raiders football uniform. The football season was a month old, and the Raiders were anxious to get him on the field. It didn't take long for the fans to see that he could still play football. In his fifth game, the Raiders faced the Seattle Seahawks. Jackson amazed the crowd with a 91-yard touchdown run. He was running so hard and so fast he didn't even stop in the end zone. He ran straight into a tunnel leading to the locker rooms. When he came out of the tunnel, he threw the football in the air and pretended to swing at it with an imaginary baseball bat.

That 91-yard touchdown run was one of the most exciting plays of the season. Nobody else in the NFL ran the ball farther in 1987. When the game was over, Bo had 221 yards and three touchdowns in eighteen carries. No Raider had ever done that before.

Bo Jackson was now an established star in two pro sports. He didn't brag much. He was too busy. By the time the football season was over, it was almost time to get ready to play baseball.

Chapter 2

Bo Jackson was born in Bessemer, Alabama, on November 30, 1962. He was the eighth child in his family. Two more were born after him. His mother, Florence Bond, and her ten children all lived in a little three-room house. She worked as a maid in a hotel. Bo's dad worked in a factory. He lived on the other side of town.

Bo's real name is Vincent Edward Jackson, but by the time he was six, he had the nickname "Boar Hog." A boar is a mean, nasty wild pig. "I was tough like a wild boar," Jackson said later. "I had one of the toughest stomachs you could imagine. My brothers would hit me and I wouldn't feel nothing."

"Boar Hog" was a long name for a little boy. Soon it was shortened to just plain "Bo." That was the name almost everybody called him. Bo didn't mind the new name. He liked it when people thought he was tough. What he didn't like was people making fun of the way he talked. Sometimes he stuttered. It was hard for him to get all the words out. Lots of times he didn't say anything so no one could hear the way he talked.

Even if he wasn't a talker, Bo was not a bashful kid. He liked to play with his brothers and sisters and cousins. He also seemed to like to get into trouble. "You name it, I did it," said Jackson. "Breaking windows, beating up kids, stealing bikes. And rock throwing — that's what I was known for. I had one guy I hit in the head two or three times a week. I was a bully."

In an interview after he became a star athlete, Bo said he took other kids' lunch money when he was in school, then loaned it back to them. He said they had to pay him back the next day with interest, or he'd beat them up. He got so rich stealing and lending money, he explained, that he paid kids to beat up people he didn't like.

Bo was so big and tough and mean that most people did whatever he told them to. "In third grade I was so bad, I'd bully the sixth graders." He later told a reporter that when his cousin tried to take his ping-pong paddle, he hit her with a baseball bat.

"I was buck wild. When I was little, every time someone got beat up, or hit in the head with a rock, or a bike was stolen or a window was broken . . . they came looking for me. I was always told, 'You're going to end up in the pen before you're 21.'"

Bo's mother tried to straighten him out. She kept telling him he would wind up in jail if he didn't start behaving himself. Bo didn't listen.

"I never lost a fight until the day I jumped this ninth grader. I was in the seventh. He hit me in the nose twice and knocked me cold." Bo decided to get even. "The next day I got my brother's .22 rifle and waited for him in this field. I had him in my sights, with the gun up to my shoulder." Just before he pulled the trigger, he started to think about what his mother had told him about going to jail. He had heard his brother talk about reform school. He didn't want to go there, either. "I took the shells out of the gun and went home."

Bo was lucky. Besides being a tough kid, he was also a very talented athlete. When he wasn't beating up other kids, he was usually beating them at sports. As a third grader, he

When he was at Auburn, Bo's biggest fans were his mother, brothers, and sisters. Here are Clarence, Janet, his mother Florence, Anthony, Jerry, Penny, and Louella.

tried out for the fourth, fifth, and sixth grade track team. "I outran everybody," he said. Even though he was too young, the coach let him join the team.

"I've been running and jumping and throwing all my life," said Jackson. "Everything comes easy to me. I really don't have to work at it." He loved playing baseball. "I played Little League for about two weeks before they decided I was too rough and moved me up to the Pony League. When I was in the Pony League, I was playing in a men's semipro league. I never played with friends my own age."

Bo might have been a great athlete, but he kept getting into trouble. When he was fourteen, he and some friends decided to go swimming. On the way to the lake, they walked past a minister's farm. He had a pen full of pigs. "We stopped and threw some rocks. One rock led to another." When Bo and his friends were done, many of the pigs were dead.

The boys were caught, and Bo's mother was mad. "My mom told the minister, 'If you want to send him to reform school, go ahead. I just can't do a thing with him.'"

Finally Bo was scared. He knew his mother and the minister meant business. He got a job and helped pay for the pigs he had killed. He finally realized it was time to change his ways. "If I'm not constantly keeping myself busy, I know I'll get in trouble." So Bo decided to stay out of trouble by playing sports. He signed up for the baseball, football, and track teams at McAdory High School in McCalla, Alabama.

When he was in ninth grade, he entered a decathlon against sixty other boys. A decathlon is a series of ten athletic events. "It was the first time I ever threw the shot or the discus or pole-vaulted." Bo finished tenth. The coaches were impressed. They were even more impressed two years later when he won the state decathlon championship. He won even though he skipped the mile race and only competed in nine of the ten events. He didn't run the mile because he didn't think it was any fun. "Distance," he said, "is the only thing I hate about track." It didn't matter. The other athletes couldn't get enough points in all ten events to beat the total he had gotten in just nine. He was the Alabama state champion two years in a row.

Bo was also the state champ in the triple jump, sometimes called "hop, step, and jump." He had to jump three times without stopping. Bo went forty-eight feet, eight and a quarter inches. When he landed on his final jump, he twisted his ankle. But that didn't stop him from coming back the next day and setting a state record in the 100-yard dash. He ran it in 9.54 seconds.

The fans who watched Bo were amazed at his talent, but they were also amused by the strange ways he did things. A discus looks like a heavy Frisbee. Athletes are taught to throw it by quickly spinning their bodies and then letting it go. Bo could throw a discus 149 feet without even spinning his body. He had just never learned the "right" way to do it.

Bo didn't do things the way he was "supposed to" in baseball, either. Sometimes he jumped up to catch balls that were coming right down to him. He just wasn't patient enough to wait.

One of the reasons Bo made a lot of mistakes on the baseball field was because he didn't have time to practice a lot. He was also on the track team. When there was a track meet, he couldn't go to baseball practice. That didn't stop him from having a .493 batting average in his senior year at McAdory or tying the national record with twenty home runs.

Bo usually played centerfield and shortstop, but sometimes his coaches had him pitch. They wanted to take advantage of his strong arm. His fastball went ninety-two miles per hour. In his senior year, he pitched two no-hitters,

When Bo was still in high school, the New York Yankees offered him a baseball contract. Years later, Bo would play against the Yankees at Royals Stadium.

but he didn't enjoy it. In fact, he thought pitching was boring. "I hated it. There's just no action. You just sit there and throw the ball." It reminded him of throwing rocks when he was a kid.

Baseball scouts from major league teams came to McCalla to watch Bo play. "He was just awesome in high school," said Ken Gonzales, who worked for the Kansas City Royals. "I was always kind of afraid he might hurt somebody, he's so strong. He's just a fascinating athlete." The scouts knew Bo Jackson had a lot of ability. With a little experience, he would get even better.

In the fall, Bo devoted all his time to football. He was almost a one-man team. When his team had the ball, Bo played halfback. When McAdory High was on defense, he played end. He also did all the kicking—kick offs, punts, field goals, and extra points. When the other team kicked off or punted, Bo was the one who returned it.

As a senior, he gained 1,173 yards. That was good enough to win a place on the all-state team. Soon people all across Alabama and the whole country were beginning to pay attention to Bo Jackson.

Pat Dye, the football coach at Auburn University, was one of the people who came to watch him play. He saw Bo knock down three men with one block. "Like dominoes," Dye said. "I never saw anything like it."

Dye wanted Jackson to play football for him at Auburn. So did coaches at colleges all over the country. But Bo didn't have to play football. He also had a chance to play major league baseball for the New York Yankees. They wanted to sign him as an outfielder.

Bo had to decide what he wanted to do. He was tempted to play for the Yankees. They offered him $250,000 to sign a contract. If he played college football, he wouldn't get any

Pat Dye was the football coach at Auburn University. He convinced Bo to play for him.

Coach Dye told Bo he would be able to play on Auburn's baseball team, too.

money. All Dye and the other coaches could offer him was a scholarship. That meant he could go to college for free.

Bo's mother was proud of her son. She liked watching him compete in sports, and she was glad he was staying out of trouble. "My mom said, 'If you want to play baseball, you do what you want,'" Jackson said, "but she wanted me to go to college." He knew that he would be the first child in his family to go to a major college. He listened to his mother and turned down the Yankees and all their money. He told Coach Dye he was coming to Auburn.

It would be fun playing football for the Auburn Tigers. Dye told him he could also be on the baseball and track teams. Bo looked forward to four exciting years. There would be time after college to play for the Yankees or some other major league baseball team. And, who knows? Maybe he'd even decide to play professional football.

Chapter 3

Going to college was a whole new way of life for Bo Jackson. He was nineteen when he enrolled in the summer of 1982. It was the first time he had ever lived apart from his mother, brothers, and sisters. Like most of the other students, Bo lived in a dormitory on campus. He missed his family.

Even before classes started, football practices began. There were usually two of them every day. The Auburn Tigers were one of the top college teams in the country. Coach Pat Dye wanted to be sure his players were ready to play. The practices were long and hard, and the Alabama weather was very hot. Bo hated going to practices every day. He knew he was a good player. He didn't think he needed to work himself so hard at practices. He didn't like the way the coaches kept yelling at the players, either.

Right after the season started, Bo decided he was tired of football and lonesome for his family. He borrowed a friend's car and headed for the Auburn bus station. He was going to buy a ticket and get on a bus for home. But when he got to the bus station, he didn't buy a ticket right away. "I started thinking of all the people back home," he said. "What if I was to just up and go home after I proved myself in high school and I proved myself up to that point? They would be disappointed in me and probably see me as one of the regular kids in the neighborhood, one of the guys that had a chance to go to college and play football, baseball, whatever, and maybe make it to the big leagues, but didn't."

Bo sat in the bus station for six hours, trying to figure out what to do. He was tired and lonesome, but he really didn't want to give up his dream of attending college. He knew how disappointed his mother would be if he quit school. He also knew he had a lot of talent. He had a chance to be one of the finest, best-known athletes in the country. He didn't want to ruin that, either. Finally, Bo decided to stay. He was going to do his best to put up with the practices and the loneliness. He got into the car and went back to his dormitory.

When he got back, he was in trouble. Football players have a curfew. That means they're supposed to be in their rooms by a certain time every night. Bo didn't get back until after midnight. The coaches told him he'd have to run up and down the steps at the football stadium for punishment. Bo didn't complain and headed for the steps the next day. He also tried to do his best at practice and not get upset when the coaches yelled.

Lionel "Little Train" James helped Jackson make it through that first year at Auburn. He and Bo were roommates in the dormitory and teammates on the football team. Having a friend made it easier to be away from home. James also gave him advice on the football field. Auburn's first opponent in 1982 was Wake Forest. Early in the game, James told Bo, "Don't be nervous. When we pitch you the ball, take off." Jackson took the advice and took off. On one play, he went down the sideline for 44 yards and a touchdown. The rest of

Bo was a starter as a freshman for the Auburn Tigers. He scored nine touchdowns that year.

the day went almost as well. Bo carried the ball ten times for 123 yards. It was a great first game for a freshman.

Jackson played well throughout the 1982 season. He gained 110 yards against Tennessee, 111 against Kentucky, and 114 against Rutgers. Going into the last game against the Alabama Crimson Tide, he had eight touchdowns and 715 yards.

Just as in every other year, the 1982 Auburn-Alabama game was one of the most important ones of the season. With only two minutes and thirty seconds left, Alabama had a 22–17 lead. Auburn had the ball on the Alabama one-yard line, but it was fourth down. Coach Pat Dye knew his team only had one chance left. He decided to give the ball to Jackson. Bo took the handoff and slammed into the Alabama line. They had him stopped, but he kept wiggling and pushing until he popped over the goal line. Auburn won 23–22.

Besides scoring the winning touchdown, Bo had also gained 114 yards against Alabama. That gave him nine touchdowns and 829 yards in 127 attempts for his first college season.

There's a unique tradition in Auburn. Whenever the team wins, the fans cover a street corner on campus with toilet paper. "When we beat 'Bama in '82," said Jackson, "they rolled the corner for two days. People bought up all the paper in town."

When the football season was over, Bo started to think about baseball. He had a lot of talent, but he needed a lot more practice and experience before he would be a really fine player. Competing with Auburn against other college teams would be a lot harder than playing for McAdory High School.

The baseball season started miserably for Jackson. In his first twenty-one tries, he struck out every time. He began to wonder if he was really good enough to play for Auburn. But

Bo didn't quit, and he got better. By the end of the season, his batting average was .279.

The major league baseball scouts still had their eyes on him. They hoped he would sign a contract someday to play for them. "His fielding was weak," said one scout, "but fielding is the easiest thing to teach, so that isn't a problem. He just has to learn the game. But the physical tools? You could scout for years and years and never see a guy like that."

One day in his freshman season, Jackson got mad and gave a hint of the kind of baseball player he could be. Auburn was playing a game in Tuscaloosa, Alabama. There was a beer truck parked on the other side of the outfield fence. The driver and his friends were drinking beer and laughing at Bo. They called him names when he played the outfield. Jackson didn't say anything. He just waited until the next time he came up to bat. He took a big swing and slammed a home run off the side of the beer truck. The driver and his friends didn't have anything else to say.

Bo Jackson was becoming one of the most popular athletes in the whole state of Alabama. After his freshman year, he got a summer job as a bank teller in Birmingham. On his way to work, he ran into the back of another car. Nobody was hurt, but the driver was mad. She told Bo that he was a lousy driver and that the accident was all his fault. Bo didn't say anything until she asked him his name. Her mouth fell open. "Are you the Bo Jackson who plays for Auburn?" she asked. "Oh, are you all right?" She had forgotten about her car. She just wanted to make sure Bo could still carry the ball for the Auburn Tigers.

Jackson left his job at the bank when football practice started late in the summer. The Auburn Tigers were hoping for an undefeated season in 1983. One of their biggest fans was the woman whose car Bo had hit. Just before the second game of the season against Texas, she sent Bo a message: "Smash Texas like you smashed my car."

The Texas game was Auburn's only loss in 1983. Coach Dye said it was his fault. He only had Bo run the ball seven times. "It was a drastic mistake," he said.

During Jackson's second year at Auburn, the coaches lightened up on him at practice. "That's when we came off him," said Bud Casey, the backfield coach. "We let him go at his own pace, whatever he felt like." The coaches had realized

Coach Dye said he made "a drastic mistake" when he let Bo run the ball only seven times against Texas.

that Bo was a special kind of athlete who didn't need rugged practices like everybody else. "I have never in my life been around an athlete like that," said Dye. "I think he has tuned that body and he knows how that body responds better than I do."

Except for the loss to Texas, Auburn had a great year in 1983. Jackson was even better than he had been as a freshman. He scored twelve touchdowns and gained 1,213 yards in 158 tries. He piled up more than 100 yards in six of the eleven games. Once again, he saved one of his best performances for the final game against Alabama. He helped Auburn take an early lead with an incredible 69-yard touchdown. This time when he ran into a line of Alabama players, he took off in the other direction and outraced them to the end zone. Late in the game, Alabama went ahead 20–16. Once again Bo saved the day. He clinched the victory by running the ball 71 yards for another touchdown. Auburn won 23–20.

After the 1983 season, Auburn went to the Sugar Bowl in New Orleans for a game against Michigan. Both teams were tough. Auburn was 10–1 and Michigan 9–2. Bo Schembechler, Michigan's coach at that time, knew he'd have to keep his eye on Jackson. "Some people think he's already the best back in college football," Schembechler said, "and from what I've seen on film I'm in no position to argue with them."

The Auburn-Michigan game was a great one. "This was the hardest, the most physical game I've played in since I came to Auburn," Bo said. Both teams had great defenses, and neither quarterback had much luck completing passes. In the last quarter, Michigan led 7–3. Then Al DelGreco kicked his second field goal of the night, and Auburn was down by just one, 7–6. After Michigan failed to move the ball, the Tigers got their last chance. Thomas Agee, Jackson, and his roommate Lionel James took turns running the ball on that last drive. Agee led the way with four carries for thirty-two yards, but Auburn stalled at the Michigan 42. It was fourth and two. Dye knew his team was too far out for DelGreco to kick another field goal. He decided to get the ball to James. Bo's friend came through. He took the ball four yards to the 38. Auburn had a first down. A few plays later, with only twenty-three seconds left, DelGreco kicked his third field goal of the game, giving Auburn a 9–7 win.

Jackson had more yardage than anybody that night. He gained 130 yards in twenty-two tries. After the game he was awarded the Most Valuable Player trophy, but he surprised everybody by turning the award over to his friend "Little Train" James, who had gained 94 yards in eighteen attempts. Jackson didn't want to have all the glory. Besides, James had made the big play when it counted. He had gotten the first down when Auburn needed to get close enough for DelGreco to attempt the game-winning field goal.

The Sugar Bowl victory against Michigan was the last football game of the 1983 season. In a few weeks, the baseball team began practicing—without Bo. He had decided to concentrate on running. The Olympics would be taking place that summer in Los Angeles. Bo had dreams of competing as a sprinter for the United States team. His best time in the 100-meter dash was 10.39 seconds. That was fast, but other runners were faster. He worked hard to improve his time, but he finally had to admit he wasn't good enough to make the U.S. Olympic team. For the first time, he was unable to achieve one of his athletic dreams.

Bo had other things on his mind besides sports. He was spending a lot of time working with other college students and young children at the Auburn Child Study Center. One of his friends was a pretty young woman named Linda. She was one of the few people who called him Vincent. "That's his real name," she said. "And I'm not real big on nicknames." Bo liked that. He also liked Linda. She cheered for him at games and encouraged him in his classwork. Linda had a lot of classwork herself. She had already graduated from college and was beginning work on her doctorate, an advanced college degree.

Soon after he met Linda, Jackson had an idea to give a lot

Bo spent many hours as a volunteer working with children at the Auburn University Child Study Center.

of kids some fun. Auburn was going to play a practice football game after several weeks of practice in the spring of 1984. Since Bo was running track, he couldn't play in the game. Instead he challenged the kids at the game to a race. If anybody could beat him from one end of the football field to the other, he would buy him supper. Hundreds of kids poured onto the field. After giving them a 15-yard headstart, Bo beat them all easily. At the edge of the field, he jumped over the fence into the stands. None of the kids got a free supper, but

Bo might have won the Heisman Trophy in 1984, but a shoulder injury kept him out of action for six games.

Bo made sure they all got autographs. He spent the rest of the night in the stands with them, talking and signing.

Jackson was back on the football field in time for summer practices as the Auburn Tigers prepared for the 1984 season. Many sports fans expected him to be a contender that year for the Heisman Trophy. He started out well, picking up 96 yards against Miami and 103 against Texas, before he suffered a

Everybody wondered if Bo would be able to make it as a major league out fielder for the Kansas City Royals.

separated shoulder. That meant he had to watch the next six games from the bench. It also meant he had no chance for the Heisman. He wasn't really back in top shape until the eleventh game of the season when he carried the ball eighteen times for 87 yards against Georgia. In the annual battle against Alabama, his 118 yards helped Auburn win again.

The Tigers closed out 1984 by playing Arkansas in the Liberty Bowl. Once again Bo got a Most Valuable Player Trophy. He had 88 yards and two touchdowns.

The 1985 baseball season was Jackson's best ever. His batting average was .401. It looked like he was becoming an experienced, smart player, not just a talented one.

Bo's last year at Auburn was the most exciting. He finally won the Heisman Trophy. By 1985, people all over the country were talking about him. Most of them thought he was just about the finest running back they'd ever seen.

His final college baseball season in the spring of 1986 didn't go nearly as smoothly. He was distracted by all the talk about the Heisman and his chances in the National Football League. His batting average was just .246. Everybody thought his baseball days were over. That's when he surprised them by turning down the NFL and signing a contract to play the outfield for the Kansas City Royals.

Many fans thought Bo had made an awful mistake. How could he give up all the money he would have made as a pro football running back? And what if he wasn't good enough to be a major league baseball player?

Bo Jackson wasn't worried. He smiled and said, "In life you take chances." He was ready to take his chances with baseball and the Kansas City Royals.

Chapter 4

A lot of people thought Bo Jackson was crazy to turn down almost $500,000 a year from the Tampa Bay Buccaneers. After all, the Kansas City Royals were only offering him $200,000 to play baseball. But other things were more important than money. Bo wanted to play baseball, and, as Auburn assistant baseball coach Ed Thayer said, "He just values being happy more than being rich."

Jackson's first stop in pro baseball wasn't Kansas City. He had to go to Memphis, Tennessee, to play for the Chicks in a Double-A minor league. The Royals wanted him to get some more experience before he tried playing in the majors. They were confident that soon he would be a major league superstar.

Jackson joined the Memphis Chicks in the summer of 1986. His arrival was big news in Memphis. More than 150 reporters showed up to cover his first game. The fans stood and cheered when he approached home plate for the first time. He didn't let them down. With two men on base, he bounced a single up the middle for his first professional hit.

Playing in the minor leagues wasn't as tough as it would have been in the majors, but it was a lot harder than playing for Auburn. After his first game, Bo had a pretty rough time. He made ten outs in a row, striking out five times. By the end of his first week in Memphis, he had struck out fourteen times and was only batting .065.

After three games as designated hitter, the Chicks decided to let him play defense, too. In his first game as a right fielder, he almost dropped an easy line drive that came right to him. He made two mistakes the next night. After getting hit by a pitch, he got picked off first base because he wasn't paying close enough attention to the pitcher's moves. Then he couldn't pick up an easy single that rolled to him in right field. That error allowed two runs to score. In his twenty-six at-bats after his first single, Jackson only got one other hit. That was a little pop up the wind blew away from a fielder. He lucked out and got a double on that one. Most of the time the pitchers were fooling him with curveballs. Then, when he looked for the curve, they'd slip him a fastball.

During his terrible slump, Bo had more to think about than baseball. On July 13, 1986, he and Linda had their first child, a boy named Garrett Lamar. Some people were surprised to hear that Bo Jackson had become a family man. He had always told his friends, "I don't want my life tied down."

But that was before he met Linda while they were both studying child development at Auburn. They loved being with kids, and, as Bo finally decided, "Coming home to an empty house is not my idea of fun." He enjoyed his new family. "When I leave the ball park, I become a father and a husband. It's a whole new job." The first thing he did when he got home was put little Garrett into his lap and talk to him. He called the baby "Spud."

Jackson didn't like being away from his family, but ball

Bo looked forward to slugging the ball in front of the hometown fans at Royals
Stadium.

players spend a lot of time on the road. They have to travel all over the country. When he was away, Bo called Linda every night. He always asked her to hold the phone up to his son's ear. "He was so funny about that," Linda said. "He was so afraid Garrett would forget the sound of his voice."

Linda and the baby were doing fine, but Bo was still having a rough time with the Memphis Chicks. Some people wondered if he would be able to make it as a pro baseball player. The late Dick Howser wasn't worried. He was the manager of the Kansas City Royals at that time. "It is true that the only thing we're overlooking is he hasn't played a lot," Howser said. With a little more experience, he was sure Bo would be just fine. Bo wasn't worried, either. "I've always got off slow in baseball," he said.

It took him a few weeks, but finally Bo got the hang of playing minor league ball. He learned to hit the tricky pitches and stopped striking out quite so much. By September, he was batting .338.

Late in the season, the Royals decided it was time to see how Jackson would do in the major leagues. Bo left the Memphis Chicks and headed for Kansas City. In his first at-bat, he faced the legendary pitcher Steve Carlton. Bo sent the first pitch sailing into the stands, but it was foul. Now that he had shown his power, he concentrated on getting on base. He beat out an infield grounder for a hit. The Royals were happy. Not only was their new player a power hitter, he was also the fastest man on the field.

Jackson's happiest moment as a 1986 Royal came when he belted a 475-foot home run over the fence at Royals Stadium. But he still had a lot to learn. In just twenty-five games with Kansas City at the end of the 1986 season, he struck out thirty-four times. His batting average was just .207. His fielding was a little shaky, and he still had trouble hitting curveballs. Some of his teammates also wondered if he was willing to work hard enough to make it in the major leagues. They didn't like the way he seemed to take it easy at practice.

After the season ended, Bo decided it was time to show his teammates how hard he was willing to work to make it with the Royals. While the rest of the team was resting during the winter, Jackson spent time with Ed Napoleon, a minor league

Bo's unique batting style soon became a familiar sight at Royals Stadium.

outfield coach. "He worked his tail off," Napoleon said. "I'd hit balls I knew he couldn't get to, and he'd go after them as hard as he could, even though he didn't really know how to go after them. He'd wait until they got through the infield, then try to get a jump. He didn't even know how to hold his glove on ground balls, which is why he missed so many. But he worked and he listened, and because he is such a great athlete, he learns fast."

In the spring, Jackson headed for the Royals training camp in Florida. His former teammate Dan Quisenberry saw the improvement. "We wondered about his work habits," he said. "Then when he got to spring training, his work habits were what struck us all." Bo spent a lot of hours on the practice field. His teammates could see he was turning into a real major leaguer. The Royals had planned to send him to another minor league team for the start of the 1987 season. But, as Royals catcher Jamie Quirk said, "By the time we broke camp, everyone knew Bo belonged in the major leagues."

Jackson was glad to be on the Kansas City Royals for good. He gave a lot of credit to Napoleon, his fielding instructor. "Without him," he said, "I wouldn't be here. He's been like a father to me."

Halfway through the first month of the 1987 season, Bo was batting .500. He had five infield singles, two doubles, and three home runs. He also had thirteen runs batted in (RBI)—more than anybody else in the American League. He got four hits and three RBI against New York on April 10. Four days later, he hit two singles and a pair of home runs, one of them a grand slam, as the Royals clobbered the Detroit Tigers, 10–1. Even Tiger manager Sparky Anderson was impressed. He'd been playing and managing baseball for more than thirty years. "Bo Jackson's the best athlete I've ever seen in a baseball uniform," Anderson said.

Bo was pleased with his start, but he wished the fans and the reporters wouldn't give him quite so much attention. "I'll be glad when I've been around the league once and I can just play baseball. For now, I just hope fans see me as a player, not a superman. As for the future, showing folks what you can do goes a whole lot further than telling."

Now that he had proved himself as a major league baseball

Pitcher Dan Quisenberry was impressed by Bo's determination to make the team.

player, Bo said he hoped people would stop asking him about football. "I enjoy making liars out of the people who say that I won't stick to baseball. I only set one goal and that was to make the team."

The Royals and Bo Jackson thought his football days were over. But, of course, they were wrong.

Tiger manager Sparky Anderson said he'd never seen anybody like Bo Jackson.

Chapter 5

Nobody could stay as hot as Bo was during the first few weeks of the 1987 baseball season. After April, he wasn't getting nearly as many hits. By May 3, he wasn't batting .300 anymore. He was still having trouble with curveballs. Even during his hot streak, he had tied a major league record by striking out five times in a game against the Yankees.

Midway through the season, even if he wasn't the best player in baseball, Bo had still proven that he deserved to be the Kansas City Royals' starting left fielder. He hit two home runs when the Royals bombed the Seattle Mariners 9–1 on June 7. Between June 13 and 19, he hit safely in seven straight games. The Kansas City fans loved him.

All that changed in July when Bo announced that he was going to play football for the Los Angeles Raiders after the baseball season ended. His Kansas City fans and teammates had expected him to stick with baseball. "I'm mad and the team's mad," said center fielder Willie Wilson. He didn't think it was fair that the Royals would allow Jackson to play football.

But Bo had already made up his mind, and the Royals had allowed him to sign the new football contract. It was something he wanted to do. The Raiders offered him $7.4 million for five seasons. That's almost a million and a half dollars a year. He was already getting $200,000 a season to play baseball for the Royals. It wasn't the money that made him decide to play football again. It was the challenge.

Even Bo had bad days. Once he struck out five times in a game.

If he could make it playing two pro sports at once, sports fans would remember Bo Jackson for a long, long time. But it wasn't going to be easy. It's hard enough to play just one pro sport. Thousands of athletes try, but only a few make it. Hardly anybody had ever tried to play two of them.

Jackson just wanted to see what he could do. If he had the talent to play two sports, shouldn't he try to do it? It wasn't as if he was running out on the Kansas City Royals. He'd still finish the 1987 season, and he'd be back to play in 1988. He wouldn't skip a single baseball game to play football. Bo talked to his teammates on the Royals. "Once they understood I was going to be a baseball player first and a football player only afterward, it was okay." He promised not to let them down.

There were still a lot of angry fans in Kansas City. For years, the Los Angeles Raiders had been the archrivals of the Kansas City Chiefs. Bo would soon be playing for the team the Kansas City fans hated most. "The Raiders of all people," said one fan. "That's the worst team in the world he could go to."

On July 18, 1987, when Jackson played his first baseball game in Kansas City after signing with the Raiders, the fans let him have it. Almost all of them stood and booed. They threw dozens of toy plastic footballs onto the field. The boos shook the stadium when Bo struck out in the third inning. He tried not to let it bother him. "I'm not out there to listen to criticism or to listen to boos. I'm out there to play ball. All that stuff goes in one ear and out the other."

But the boos turned to cheers in the fifth inning. Baltimore's Cal Ripkin, Jr., hit a sinking line drive into left field. Jackson could have played it on a hop for a single, but instead he turned on the speed, dove for the ball, and caught it on the ground. The cheers got even louder a moment later

Like all the other major league ball players, Bo got his own baseball card.

when Ray Knight blasted the ball over Bo's head. Jackson turned around and raced all the way to the fence before he caught it. The stadium shook with cheers when a fan tossed him another toy football as he ran to the dugout. Bo grabbed it with bare hand and slammed it to the ground. The fans loved it.

For the rest of the season, Jackson looked good in left field. He was a better fielder than he had ever been. It was his hitting that gave him the most trouble. He batted just .193 while hitting four home runs and getting eight RBI. In the last two months of the season, he only got five hits. He struck out 158 times in 1987, more than any other Royal.

Bo was disappointed when the baseball season ended on October 4. He had wanted to do better. He wished he had stayed as hot as he had been in April, but there was no time to mope. The football season was already more than a month old. It was time to take off the Royals uniform and put on one for the Los Angeles Raiders.

Jackson started slowly in the NFL. In his first game on November 1, he carried the ball only eight times for just thirty-seven yards. The Raiders lost the first four games he played. By the time they went to Seattle to play the Seahawks on November 30, they were 4–7. The Seahawks were having a fine year. They had won seven games and were in second place in the AFC West Division. The Seahawks expected to have an easy time against the Los Angeles Raiders.

But November 30, 1987, was a special day for Bo Jackson. It was his twenty-fifth birthday. It was also the day he learned Linda was pregnant with their second child. And that night against the Seahawks, Bo finally showed what he could do on a pro football field. It was a Monday night game, and the whole country was watching on national television.

Bo helped the Raiders clobber the Seahawks 37–14. He

Bo keeps his balance and picks up a big gain for the Raiders.

had a fumble early in the game that led to a Seahawk touchdown, but after that he was flawless. He scored three touchdowns and gained 221 yards.

Early in the second quarter, Jackson went around left end from his own 9-yard line. "I saw the defender had the angle so I just threw my head back" and took off, Bo said. After he turned on the speed, nobody came close. When he crossed the goal line ninety-one yards later, no Seahawk player was within five yards of him. Jackson's speed wasn't what saved him in the third quarter when he ran into Seattle's big linebacker Brian Bosworth two yards from the end zone. Bo had to use his great strength to carry Bosworth with him across the goal line.

ABC–TV announcer Al Michaels thought Jackson was awesome. "It looked like a grown man playing against boys," he said. Of course, Bo really enjoyed himself. "It was just one of those nights when you can do nothing wrong and the other team can do nothing right," he said. Now all the reporters wanted to know if he was going to give up baseball to concentrate on football. It was still hard for them to believe he could play both sports. "I hadn't thought about it," Bo said. "Why should I think about it? I'm having too much fun."

Bo was ready to have some more fun two weeks later when the Raiders went to Kansas City to play the Chiefs. The game was in Arrowhead Stadium just across the parking lot from Royals Stadium, where he had played baseball all summer. The Kansas City fans were ready for him, and most of them were still mad that he had decided to play football for the Raiders. There were 63,834 people in Arrowhead Stadium that night. They had brought more than 100 signs and banners making fun of Jackson. They wanted to see their Chiefs chew up Bo and his new team. But the first time he carried the ball, Jackson sprained his right ankle and started limping. He was

Bo was the first athlete in a long, long time to be on a football card and a baseball card in the same year.

only able to run the ball two more times before he hobbled over to the bench where he stayed the rest of the game. Without Bo, the Raiders lost 16–10.

Jackson's ankle injury wasn't serious, but it didn't heal in time for him to play in either of the Raiders' final two games. That meant he finished his first pro football season with four touchdowns and 554 yards in eighty-one carries. That's an average of 6.8 yards a carry. He also caught sixteen passes for 136 yards and two more touchdowns.

After the season ended, sports historian L. Robert Davids did some research. He discovered that before Jackson, only four pro athletes had ever hit a home run in baseball and scored a touchdown in football during the same year. Until 1987, the best anybody had ever done was two homers and two touchdowns. Bo Jackson did a lot better than that. He slammed twenty-two home runs for the Royals, then scored six touchdowns for the Raiders.

So 1987 had been a very interesting year. Bo had hit long home runs, set records in two sports, made dazzling catches, and run for touchdowns. People all over the country were talking about him. He hoped he would do even better in 1988.

Chapter 6

When the football season ended, the Jackson family moved back to Kansas City from California. Bo had only a few weeks' rest before it was time to take Linda and Garrett to Florida for baseball spring training.

Jackson had another good baseball year in 1988. During May, he batted .330 with five home runs, nineteen RBI, and nine stolen bases. He was named the Royals' Player of the Month. His fielding was sharp, too. During the first two months of the season, he threw out nine runners from his spot in the outfield.

The baseball season was interrupted by a happy moment in August. "Spud" got a baby brother, Nicholas. Bo was in the delivery room with Linda. When he held his new son for the first time, he was so happy he cried. "I could see the look on the nurse's face," said Linda. "She was shocked that this was Bo Jackson, that he was so human and so nice."

The nurse wasn't the only one who noticed that Bo was a nice guy. He was popular with fans across the country. Many top athletes won't sign autographs unless they're paid. Not

Bo. "He says he won't make a kid pay for an autograph," said his agent Richard Woods. "I've seen him stand three hours signing autographs after a game." Jackson's also popular with the boys who work in the players' locker room. He gives each of them a tip. "Not only that," says Don Fitzpatrick, who works at Boston's Fenway Park, "but he talks to each of them about staying in school, staying away from drugs, trying to do something for society. Bo's special."

Bo cuddles his three-month-old son Nicholas.

But even nice guys get injured. Late in the 1988 baseball season, Bo suffered a torn left hamstring muscle that kept him out of action for a month. He still finished the year with twenty-five homers, sixty-eight RBI, and twenty-seven stolen bases. He was also the first Royal ever to hit as many as twenty-five homers while stealing more than twenty-five bases the same year.

Bo's torn hamstring had healed by the time he was ready to play football again. Mike Shanahan, the new Raider coach, was happy to have Bo in the lineup. "Any time you have the type of player who can score a touchdown on every play or make a big play on every play, it's got to have an influence on the team," he said.

Jackson's first appearance was in Kansas City where the Raiders played the Chiefs. The stadium was filled. Bo didn't let Shanahan down. He gained seventy yards and scored a touchdown as the Raiders won 27–17.

The next week against New Orleans, Jackson looked hotter than ever. He ran twenty-five yards the first time he got the ball. The next time he broke loose for twenty. The Saints couldn't stop him, but a pulled hamstring muscle did. Bo had to come out of the game in the first quarter. The Raiders lost 20–6.

When the Chiefs came to Los Angeles, Jackson was back in action. He and Marcus Allen scored touchdowns as the Raiders won 17–10. A week later, Allen had sixty-seven yards and Jackson sixty-four as the Raiders beat San Diego 13–3.

Bo was looking forward to another big game against the Seattle Seahawks late in the season. Everybody remembered the 221 yards he got against them in 1987. This time the Seahawks were ready. They concentrated on Bo. Every time he got the ball, he was surrounded. He only gained thirty-one yards in thirteen carries. After the game, Seattle strong safety

Paul Moyer said, "The secret for us was to string him out and gang tackle him." Seattle won 35–27.

After Bo rejoined the Raiders, they won five of their last ten games. They finished the 1988 season with a 7–9 mark. Jackson had some impressive statistics. He gained 513 yards and scored three touchdowns.

By 1989, Bo Jackson was probably the most famous athlete in America. When fans weren't watching him sock homers for the Royals or score touchdowns for the Raiders, they saw him star in a series of commercials for the Nike sportswear company. Rock 'n' roller Bo Diddley, basketball great Michael Jordan, and hockey superstar Wayne Gretzky teamed up with Bo in one of them.

Jackson was fast becoming an even better baseball player. In 1989, he belted thirty-two homers and knocked in 105 runs, his best totals yet. When he approached the plate, the fans began chanting, "Bo... Bo... Bo." Even the other players were anxious to see what he could do. "Bo is the only baseball player that you sense can do whatever he wants," said Willie Wilson, the Royals center fielder. "And you can't wait to see him do it."

Jackson was getting better by getting smarter. He watched the opposing pitchers closely and tried to learn from his mistakes. Early in May, Nolan Ryan, the great Texas Ranger pitcher, struck him out four times in a game. "It was fun," Ryan said. "I just reared back and threw as hard as I could, and he swung as hard as he could." Twelve days later, in Texas, Ryan again faced Jackson. The first two times up, he struck him out again. But Bo hung in there, and on his third time up, he blasted the ball into the center field bleachers, 461 feet away. It was the longest ball ever hit at Arlington Stadium.

Boston's Roger Clemens was another pitcher who had

given Jackson a lot of trouble. He'd struck him out nine of thirteen tries. Bo wasn't one to give up. When Clemens faced the Royals early in the season, Jackson said, "I'm going to get him." Clemens wasn't worried. When Bo came up, the Boston star let loose a fastball. "He'd never shown that he could hit that pitch," Clemens said. This time was different. "He whistled his bat through the strike zone like nothing I'd ever

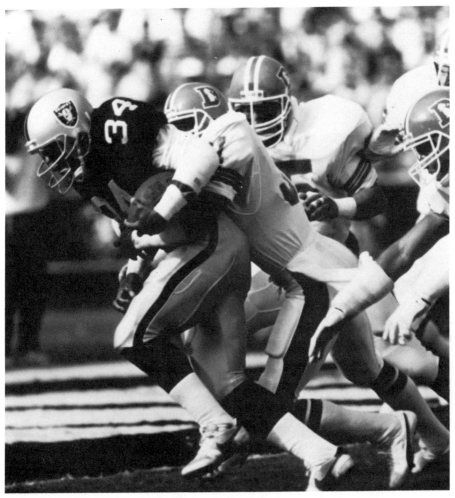

Bo takes off against the Denver Broncos.

seen, and he hit the ball so hard I couldn't even turn around to see it go over the fence."

But Bo's biggest baseball moment of 1989 came when he played his first All-Star Game. The fans elected him to the team with more votes than any other American League player. He didn't let them down. He led off the first inning by blasting a 448-foot home run into the center field bleachers at Anaheim Stadium. "When the bat hit the ball, it sounded like he hit a golf ball" said National League manager Tommy Lasorda. "He's awesome."

In the second inning, Bo put the American League ahead to stay by knocking in a run. A few pitches later, he stole second base. That made him the second player in baseball history to hit a homer and steal a base in the same All-Star Game. The only other man to do it was Willie Mays. The American League won 5–3, and Jackson was named the game's Most Valuable Player.

Everybody was impressed with Bo's All-Star performance. "He's a human highlight film," said Kirby Puckett, the great Minnesota Twin outfielder. Wade Boggs, of the Boston Red Sox, was amazed by Bo's homer. "When he hit it, I thought, 'Oh, my gosh,' " said Boggs. "It was a sight to see."

Once again, Jackson didn't do a lot of bragging. "I got a piece of it" was all he would say about the home run. He got tired of people comparing him to superstars of the past. "I really hate it when people call me the next Willie Mays or the next Babe Ruth. People should be judged on what they do, not what other people have done."

Bo's thirty-two homers for 1989 put him fourth in the American League. His .256 batting average was his highest ever. He knocked in a run every 4.9 trips to the plate. That was the best RBI ratio in the league. But Jackson also led the

Bo comes up from his slide into second base with another stolen base to his credit.

league with 172 strikeouts. You couldn't miss his name in the baseball statistics.

Bo also piled up the most impressive football statistics of his pro career in 1989. Even though he joined the Los Angeles Raiders a month into the season, he gained 950 yards in 173 carries.

In one of his first games, he picked up eighty-five yards and scored a touchdown to lead the Raiders past the Kansas City Chiefs 20–14. "I had a whole lot of fun today," Jackson said. "It was like playing against my neighbors." The Chiefs, of course, play their home games in Arrowhead Stadium, right across the parking lot from Royals Stadium, where Bo's team plays baseball during the summer. "I know all the guys on the Chiefs. In fact, a couple of them came over for dinner last night."

Two weeks later, the Raiders beat the Washington Redskins 37–24 as Bo picked up 144 yards in nineteen carries. His longest run of the day was good for 73 yards and a touchdown.

Jackson made National Football League history when the Raiders dumped the Cincinnati Bengals 28–7. He took a handoff at his own eight-yard line and raced ninety-two yards for a touchdown. That made him the first NFL player to score two touchdowns on runs longer than ninety yards. He finished the game with 159 yards in thirteen carries. When the season ended, Bo finally had a vacation. He had two months before the start of baseball's spring training. Instead of playing in stadiums in front of thousands of people, he spent quiet time with his family and kept his legs in shape by taking walks with his wife.

Bo began 1990 batting .272 with 28 home runs and 78 RBIs for the Kansas City Royals. That year, he also had another all-star football season. He became the first running back to run twice for touchdowns longer than 90 yards.

But, on January 13, 1990, tragedy struck. Jackson sustained an injury to his left hip while playing for the Raiders. The injury ended Bo's days as the star running back of the Los Angeles Raiders, but it did not end his baseball career. After being released by the Kansas City Royals, Bo joined the Chicago White Sox.

Because his hip was slow to heal, Jackson gave up stealing bases and playing in the outfield. In 1991, he only played in 23 games as a designated hitter for the White Sox, earning a respectable batting average of .225. By the end of the 1991 season, Bo's hip still had not healed properly. He underwent hip replacement surgery, and missed the entire 1992 season.

Many people, including Bo's trainers and coaches, were unsure if Bo could bounce back from his surgery and play with an artificial hip. But Bo made a miraculous recovery, and helped the White Sox clinch the division title in 1993.

For the 1994 season, Bo signed with the California Angels. Playing as a designated hitter, Bo lifted his batting average to .279. Once again, though, Bo was off the field before the season was over. On September 14, 1994, the major league baseball players went on strike.

Bo had already decided what he would do when his sports career was over. He retired from professional sports in April 1995. Since then he has received his degree in child development from Auburn. Bo has also kept busy by opening a shop that customizes motorcycles, overseeing an Alabama restaurant, and even doing some acting.

Although Bo won't have big crowds to cheer for him anymore, he'll still be doing important work. And it will be a job that he loves.

CAREER STATISTICS

FOOTBALL CAREER RECORD

YEAR	CLUB	CARRIES	YARDS	AVG. YARDS	TOUCH-DOWNS
1982	Auburn	127	829	6.5	9
1983	Auburn	158	1213	7.7	12
1984	Auburn	87	475	5.5	5
1985	Auburn	278	1786	6.4	17
1986	——	—	—	—	—
1987	Raiders	81	554	6.8	4
1988	Raiders	136	580	4.3	3
1989	Raiders	173	950	5.5	4
1990	Raiders	125	698	5.6	5

BASEBALL CAREER RECORD

YEAR	CLUB	G	AB	R	H	2B	3B	HR	RBI	SB	AVG.
1986	Memphis	53	184	30	51	9	3	7	25	3	.277
1986	Royals	25	82	9	17	2	1	2	9	3	.207
1987	Royals	116	396	46	93	17	2	22	53	10	.235
1988	Royals	124	439	63	108	16	4	25	68	27	.246
1989	Royals	135	515	86	132	15	6	32	105	26	.256
1990	Royals	111	405	74	110	16	1	28	78	15	.272
1991	White Sox	23	71	8	16	4	0	3	14	0	.225
1992	——	—	—	—	—	—	—	—	—	—	—
1993	White Sox	85	284	32	66	9	0	16	45	0	.232
1994	Angels	75	201	23	56	7	0	13	43	1	.279
Major League Totals		694	2393	341	698	86	14	141	415	82	.250

Index

Little League, 17
Long, Chuck, 7, 8
Los Angeles Raiders, 11-13,
    44-52, 55-56, 60, 62

M
Mays, Willie, 58
McAdory High School, 9,
    17-20, 27
Memphis Chicks, 11, 36-39,
    61, 62
Miami, University of, 34
Michaels, Al, 50
Michigan State University, 7
Michigan, University of, 30-31
Minnesota Twins, 58
Moyer, Paul, 55-56

N
Napoleon, Ed, 40-41
New Orleans Saints, 55
New York Yankees, 19, 20-23,
    44

O
Olympics, 31

P
Pony League, 17
Puckett, Kirby, 58

Q
Quirk, Jamie, 41
Quisenberry, Dan, 41, 42

R
Ripkin, Cal, Jr., 46
Royals Stadium, 11, 19, 38,
    39, 40, 50, 60
Ruth, Babe, 58
Ryan, Nolan, 56

S
Schembechler, Bo, 30
Seattle Mariners, 44

Seattle Seahawks, 13, 48-50,
    55
Shanahan, Mike, 55
Southern Mississippi,
    University of, 5
Southwest Louisiana
    University, 5

T
Tampa Bay Buccaneers, 7, 9,
    11, 36
Tennessee, University of, 5, 27
Texas Rangers, 56
Texas, University of, 28-29,
    30, 34
Tiffin, Van, 7

W
Wake Forest University, 25-27
Washington Redskins, 60
White, Lorenzo, 7
Wilson, Willie, 44, 56
Woods, Richard, 54